MILL CREEK SCHOOL
ELEM MEDIA CENTER

A/R

DISTRICT
OF COLUMBIA

in words and pictures

BY KATHRYN WENTZEL LUMLEY

ILLUSTRATIONS BY RICHARD WAHL

Consultant:
Sandra L. Burch
Smithsonian Institution

CHILDRENS PRESS ®
CHICAGO

For John and Joe Lumley, Margaret McNamara, Jaime Lane,
F.W. Heaton, and the staff and students of the D.C. Public Schools.

Downtown Washington, D.C., with the Capitol in the background

Library of Congress Cataloging in Publication Data

Lumley, Kathryn Wentzel.
    District of Columbia in words and pictures.

    SUMMARY: Surveys the history, important sites,
and prominent people of the District of Columbia.
    1. Washington, D.C.—Juvenile literature.
[1. Washington, D.C.]   I. Wahl, Richard, 1939-
II. Title.
F194.3.L85   975.3   80-39645
ISBN 0-516-03951-2

Copyright© 1981 by Regensteiner Publishing Enterprises, Inc.
All rights reserved. Published simultaneously in Canada.
Printed in the United States of America.

        6 7 8 9 10 R 89 88 87 86 85

Picture Acknowledgments:

WASHINGTON, D.C., CONVENTION AND VISITORS' ASSOCIATION—2,
21 (3), 23 (above right), 24, 25 (2), 26, 27 (2), 28, 29 (3), 30 (2), 31, 32
(2), 33 (right), 34 (2), 35, 42 (4), 45
SMITHSONIAN INSTITUTION—National Museum of American History,
37; National Air and Space Museum, 39 (2); National Zoo, 41 (4)
UNITED STATES POSTAL SERVICE—6
USDI, NATIONAL PARK SERVICE George Washington Parkway, Turkey
Run Park—8
LIBRARY OF CONGRESS—19
THE NATIONAL SHRINE OF THE IMMACULATE CONCEPTION—23
(bottom)
WASHINGTON CATHEDRAL—23 (top)
FORD'S THEATRE—33
JOHN F. KENNEDY CENTER PHOTO DEPARTMENT, Jack Buxbaum—44
UNIPHOTO: Robert M. Anderson—9

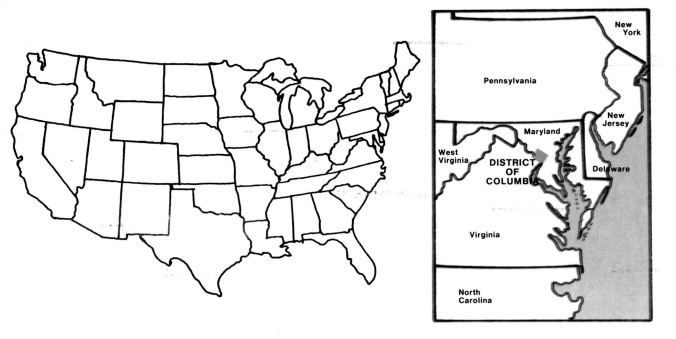

Washington, D.C., is the capital of the United States. It is one of the most unusual cities in the world. Washington was built to be the home of our federal government. It is a city that has no state. It is a district — the District of Columbia. The district was made from land given by Maryland and Virginia.

Do you know where the largest library in the world is located? Do you know where the FBI has its headquarters? Do you know where the paper money issued by our government is printed? Do you know where the Cherry Blossom Festival is held every spring? Do you know where Samuel F.B. Morse was when he sent the world's first telegraph message?

The answers to these questions are found in Washington, D.C. You will enjoy learning about the many things that happened in this exciting city that tells the history of our country.

Thousands of years ago a large part of what is now the District of Columbia was made up of swamplands. Tropical plants and animals lived in them. Years later when the Mayflower Hotel was being built, part of a cypress swamp was uncovered. This swamp must have covered a big part of what is now downtown Washington. What a change from swamps to today's wide streets, beautiful buildings, monuments, and parks!

For years the land in the district kept sinking. Water birds lived where sheep used to graze. But all that has stopped now. The land in Washington has not changed in many years.

Can you imagine a dinosaur walking around our
nation's capital? That is exactly what they used to do.
That was years before it was our nation's capital with
people living there. The dinosaurs liked the tropical
swamplands. Now they can be seen in Washington only
in the Smithsonian Institution. Occasionally, dinosaur
bones are dug out of the ground around the district.

The land now known as the District of Columbia has a lot of variety within its 68 square miles. There are two islands, a canal, a creek, and two rivers. The weather ranges from an all-time low of 15 degrees below zero to an all-time high of 106 degrees. There is something for everyone in Washington, D.C.

Falls on the Potomac River

The Potomac (pah • TOH • mick) River and the Anacostia (an • ah • COSS • tya) River flow through the district. The Potomac is both popular and important. It is so much a part of Washington that people who love the city and do not want to leave it are said to have "Potomac Fever." The Potomac is not very close to the ocean but it often has tides that are three feet high.

Rock Creek is a large, lovely stream that just misses being big enough to be a river. Thousands of years ago mountain ranges stood where it flows. Now there are huge rocks and ledges around the creek. They were left from the old mountain ranges. Rock Creek flows through Rock Creek Park right in the heart of Washington. The Creek keeps the area cool during the hot summer. Rock Creek and the park provide beauty for picnickers and nature lovers.

Statue of Theodore Roosevelt on Roosevelt Island

Columbia (co • LUM • bee • ah) Island and Roosevelt
(ROOZ • eh • velt) Island are both in the Potomac River.
Theodore Roosevelt Memorial Island is a nature area.
The National Park Service is in charge of it. Birds,
animals, and plants live in this wilderness area. No
cars are ever allowed on the island. There is now a statue
of President Roosevelt because the island park is named
in his honor.

Hikers walk along the C&O Canal

The Chesapeake (CHESS • ah • peek) and Ohio Canal is not used for travel anymore. The canal was started in 1828. It was planned to provide a water route from the Potomac to Ohio. President John Quincy Adams turned the first spadeful of earth to begin this canal. The canal never reached Ohio, but it was important for trading. It did reach Cumberland, Maryland. The canal was used until the railroads took away most of the business. The C & O Canal is still loved by Washingtonians and visitors. It is a popular trail and recreation area.

Very little is known about the earliest settlers in the District of Columbia. No sign of large prehistoric villages has been found in the district. Still, historians think that the area was important to prehistoric people. They used the stones found here to make weapons. The Smithsonian Institution reports that great boulder quarries and workshops were along the banks of Piney Branch.

These same stone quarries were used by the Indians during historic times. The Indians dug out quartzite stones. They made them into knife blades, arrowheads, and other tools.

There were never very many Indians living in the Washington area at any one time. Most of those who did live there were Algonquin (al • GONG • kwin) Indians from the Piscataway (pis • KAT • ah • way) tribe. Missionaries found that the Piscataway chiefs ruled the land for more than fifty miles around the district. The rules of these tribal chieftains lasted for thirteen generations.

These Algonquin Indians made fish nets, baskets, materials for their homes, and other things they needed. The pottery they made was useful but not beautiful.

Another Algonquin Indian tribe was the Powhatan (poe • HAH • tahn). They had a village at what is now the foot of Capitol Hill. This hill is about 90 feet above the Potomac River. This is 50 feet higher than the land on which most of the other government buildings are located.

The Powhatans made their laws in a council house.
Now Congress makes our laws on almost this same spot.

By the year 1675 most of the Indians had died or left the District Area.

Today people from every state, and most nations, either live, or visit, in the District of Columbia. But it was not always this way. It is believed by many that the first European to visit the area was Captain John Smith. He left his Jamestown Colony in Virginia to explore the Chesapeake Bay. He sailed up the Potomac River to Little Falls. This is the spot at the District Line where the Potomac gets narrower and the water goes through a gorge of about 250 feet. Little Falls, where Captain John Smith stopped, is enjoyed by many visitors every day for its beauty.

In 1609 a young boy, Harry Spelman (SPELL • man), ran away from his father and came to America. His father was an English Lord, Sir Henry Spelman. Young Harry made friends with the Indians in the Potomac region. He became an Indian translator and trader. When a famine hit the colony of Jamestown, Harry Spelman tried to help. He sailed with Captain Henry Fleete in 1622. They went to Little Falls to buy food from the Indians to help the starving colonists. What was later to be known as George Town (now Georgetown) was then called Tohoga. It was an Indian village built so the Indians could trade on both the upper and lower Potomac River.

When Captain Fleete and Spelman went on shore at Tohoga a terrible thing happened! Harry Spelman was beheaded, most of the crew were killed, and Captain Fleete was taken captive. Captain Fleete then was forced to live with the Indians and learn their ways. He is believed to have been the first European to live in what is the District of Columbia. He talked about the good fishing, the good soil for growing food, and the fine climate of the area. He reported that buffalo, deer, bears, and turkeys were in the woods. It is hard to imagine these animals living in the area of fine homes now called Georgetown.

After Captain Fleete was ransomed he went back to England. Later he came back to Tohoga (Georgetown) and set up a trading post. This was the first business in the District of Columbia.

In the years after Captain Fleete set up his trading post more and more people came to live in the district area. Scottish immigrants settled along the Potomac in 1745. Before long George Town (once Tohoga) grew into the most important seaport in the region. It was a great tobacco market. During the Revolutionary War Georgetown was important as a supply base. The finest gun foundry in America was there.

Visitors to Georgetown today find that most of the homes and shops look very much like they did hundreds of years ago in the 1700s.

After the Revolutionary War, the government of the new United States met in eight different cities. Then the people who wrote the Constitution made a big decision. This government would have a new capital city. It would be a federal city that would not be part of any state, and it would be ruled by Congress. This new nation was able to build its capital any place the Congress picked. For a while this was a problem. States in both the North and the South wanted the capital.

It was not easy to pick a place for this new capital. But finally, President George Washington signed a bill to build the capital along the Potomac River. Washington picked the location. The District of Columbia was made from land given by Maryland and Virginia on either side of the Potomac.

Pierre L'Enfant (pee • EHR lon • FAHNT), a French engineer and architect, offered to plan the new city. President Washington accepted. Washington and L'Enfant planned a city that would be large and beautiful.

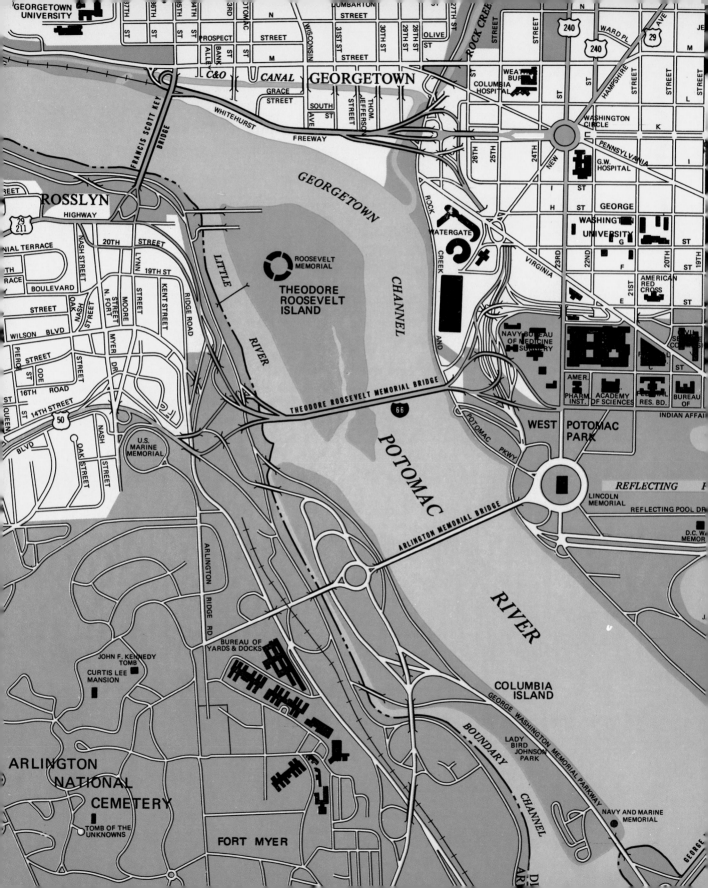

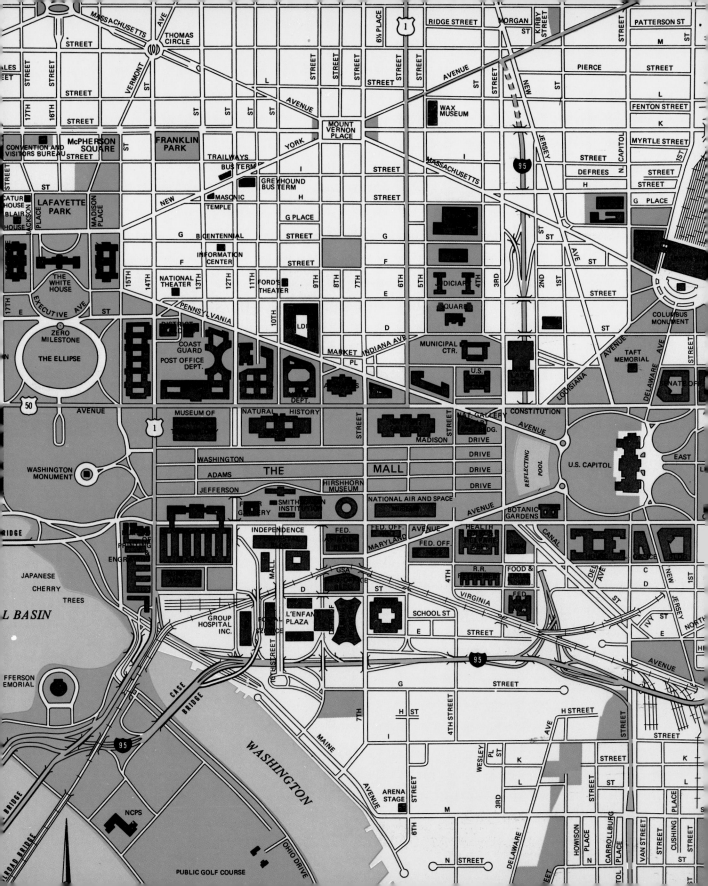

The city would have wide streets, parks, and beautiful buildings. But before the plans were really under way L'Enfant had trouble with some landowners. He was asked to leave the project.

L'Enfant returned to France. His work was taken over by Benjamin Latrobe (BEN • jah • min la • TROBE) and a black American, Benjamin Banneker (BAN • eck • er). Despite their work, it would be more than a hundred years before L'Enfant's plan for the federal city would be completed.

On September 18, 1793, President Washington laid the cornerstone for the Capitol. This building would be the home of Congress.

A slightly changed copy of William Thornton's design for the Capitol.
His original design was lost.

The committee to plan the Capitol offered a prize of $500.00 for the best plan. William Thornton from the West Indies won. Part of the Capitol still looks the way Thornton planned it.

A hill ninety feet above the Potomac was chosen for the Capitol building. It took a long time to finish the building. Washington decided not to run for another term as president. He never lived to see the Capitol or any public building completed in the city that was named for him. But the city of Washington is the finest memorial that our first president could have!

You have read about the history of the District of Columbia and the beginning of our capital city, Washington. Now it is time to take a trip—in words and pictures—through Washington, D.C.

Washington is filled with memorials, statues, and buildings that tell the history of our great country.

The president of the United States is the best-known resident of Washington. The home of the president is called the White House. It has the famous address of 1600 Pennsylvania Avenue.

When it was first built, the president's home was known as the "President's House " and the "President's Palace." During the War of 1812 the British set fire to it. It looked terrible. Then its walls were whitewashed to make them look better until they could be repaired. That is when it was given the name the White House.

The family rooms are private, but visitors are welcome to visit the East Wing. On tour days there are long lines of people waiting to visit the White House.

MILL CREEK SCHOOL
ELEM MEDIA CENTER

Above left: The south face of the White House
Above: Oval Office of the President of
      the United States
Left: The north entrance to the White House

Even the lawn of the White House is important.

On the lawn of the White House is the Zero Milestone.
All distances on United States highways are measured
from this point.

Sometimes when the president leaves the White House
he flies off in his helicopter from the south lawn. The
only time the public can use this lawn is when children
come for the annual Easter Egg Rolling.

Across from the White House is a church called the "Church of Presidents." It is St. John's Episcopal Church. One pew is marked as "The President's Pew." Every president since James Madison has been to this church at some time. Two of the windows in the north gallery are marked as "The President's Windows" to honor these famous people.

The Washington Cathedral is probably the best-known church in Washington. It has no membership of its own but is kept as "a House of Prayer for all People." It is a national church.

The largest church in the United States is in Washington. It is the National Shrine of the Immaculate Conception (im • MACK • you • let con • SEP • shun).

Above: Aerial view of Washington Cathedral and its interior
Below: The entrance to the National Shrine and its main church

23

The Capitol is the meetingplace for both the Senate and the House of Representatives of the United States.

When people in Washington talk about "The Hill" they mean Capitol Hill. Congress meets there to make the laws that govern all Americans.

Every four years the president of the United States is elected by the people. The president takes the oath of office on the east steps of the Capitol.

A statue of the Goddess of Freedom is on the top of the Capitol. When Congress is meeting there is a light in the statue.

Above: Statuary Hall in the Capitol has statues of famous Americans.
Left: The dome of the Capitol is lit at night.

There was a time during the Civil War when bread, not laws, was made in the Capitol. Part of the building was also used as a hospital.

Samuel F.B. Morse was in the basement of the Capitol when he sent the world's first telegraph message.

The senators meet in the north wing of the Capitol. The representatives meet in the south wing. Their offices are in other buildings nearby. A subway was built to bring the senators from the office building to the Capitol. The representatives have to walk. For a long time the senators had the only subway in Washington. All that is changed now. Washington has a subway to help people travel around the District.

Above: The Declaration of Independence, the Constitution of the United States, and the Bill of Rights are on display at the National Archives Building.
Right: The Library of Congress is the world's largest library.

The Library of Congress used to be part of the Capitol building. Today it is the *largest library in the world!* It is a beautiful building with 2,000 windows. Here you can see the first book that was ever printed, the Gutenberg (GOO • ten • berg) Bible. It is hard to believe that the library has nearly 275 miles of shelving with 40 million books and items on them. People come from all over the world to use the Library of Congress.

The United States Supreme Court, the highest court in the nation, is on "The Hill", too. It looks like a Greek temple with its white marble pillars. Before they had this special building, the Supreme Court used to meet in the Capitol. There are nine judges called justices. Each one is selected by the president of the United States. When the senate agrees with the president's choice, the justice is appointed. Justices are appointed for life. One of the justices serves as the Chief Justice. You can tour the Supreme Court Building when court is not in session.

The Supreme Court building and its statue that represents Justice

Washington's Japanese cherry trees in bloom

Washington is always beautiful, but in spring it has something that makes it very special. It is cherry blossom time. The city of Tokyo (TOE • kee • oh), Japan, sent more than 3,000 flowering cherry trees to the United States in 1912. They bloom in March or April when the weather gets warm. The Tidal Basin along the Potomac River is a pink-and-white picture.

Every year a Cherry Blossom Festival is held. But the blossoms do not always appear at the same time as the festival. The city fathers set the date for the festival, but Mother Nature decides when the flowers will bloom!

In the heart of Washington there is a mile and a half of parkland known as "The Mall." The Mall has famous memorials and monuments on it. These interesting reminders of our history bring millions of people to Washington. Every year five times more people come to visit than there are residents living in the city. Tourism is one of Washington's most important businesses. The other, and most important, is government. Most people in the District work for the government.

Three places to visit on the Mall: The National Gallery of Art (above left), the Smithsonian Institution's original museum building (below left), and the National Museum of American History, one of the Smithsonian buildings

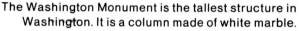
The Washington Monument is the tallest structure in Washington. It is a column made of white marble.

The Washington Monument, the best-known landmark in Washington, is in the center of the Mall. Standing over 555 feet high, it can be seen from almost any spot in the city. It is the tallest building in Washington. From the top, which you can reach by elevator, you can see beautiful sights as you look out over the four sides of the city. If you walk to the top you will go up 898 steps. Everyone enjoys this beautiful monument to the memory of our first president.

Today the Museum of African Art is in Frederick Douglass's house.

Another great panoramic (all-around) view of the city can be seen from the park around Cedar Hill. Cedar Hill is the home of the famous black leader, orator, and writer, Frederick Douglass. His home looks just like it did when he lived there, and it has his furniture and books inside. Frederick Douglass spent his life helping people.

The Anacostia Neighborhood Museum is near Cedar Hill. It is named for the Anacostia River. Young people come to learn about black history and African cultures, and to enjoy its wonderful exhibits.

The Lincoln Memorial has a marble statue of Abraham Lincoln inside it. The statue was carved by Daniel French.

One of the most popular memorials is a tribute to President Abraham Lincoln. It is a marble memorial with 36 columns around the outside. This is the number of states in the Union at the end of the Civil War.

When you climb the stairs of the Lincoln Memorial you will face a statue of President Lincoln seated on a huge marble chair. It is very impressive.

Parts of Lincoln's Second Inaugural Address and the famous Gettysburg Address are written on the walls. The Angel of Truth is shown freeing the slaves.

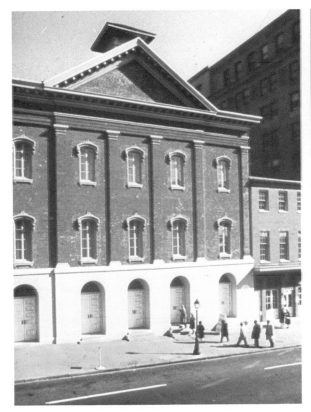

Above: The box where President Lincoln was
sitting when he was shot
Left: The front of Ford's Theatre as it
looks today

Outside the memorial the Reflecting Pool completes a
great picture by reflecting the Washington Monument on
a very clear day.

President Lincoln was assassinated (killed) on April
14, 1865, in Ford's Theatre. He and Mrs. Lincoln were in
the presidential box (seat) watching a play when he was
shot. He died in the Petersen House nearby. Both this
house and the theatre are now national museums. On
certain days of the week you can watch a play in Ford's
Theatre.

The Jefferson Memorial has a famous saying of Thomas Jefferson carved under its dome: "I have sworn upon the altar of God eternal hostility against every form of tyranny over the mind of man."

The memorial to honor President Thomas Jefferson is built in the same style as was his own home in Virginia, Monticello (mon • tih • SELL • oh). Inside there is a 19-foot bronze statue of Jefferson. He is shown standing wearing a long, fur-lined coat.

Jefferson was one of the founding fathers of our country. He was the author of the Declaration of Independence, and the third president of the United States.

The F.B.I., Federal Bureau of Investigation, has one of the most popular tours in Washington. When you tour the F.B.I. Headquarters, you learn how they solved some of their most famous cases. They have millions of

The Treasury Building

fingerprints on file. No two people ever have the same prints—not even twins. While you are there you can see pictures of the "Ten Most Wanted Criminals." There is a lot to see and learn at the headquarters of the F.B.I.

Would you like to see where all the paper money that is issued by our government is printed? At the Bureau of Engraving and Printing you can watch the bills being made, beginning with the blank paper and ending with the money the way we use it. Postage stamps are made here, too. More than nine million bills are printed every day. That is about fifty million dollars. This is the third most popular building that Washington tourists visit.

The Smithsonian Institution is made up of many things—museums, art galleries, and the National Zoo, to name a few.

This "Castle" building looks as if it should be in a foreign country, but it is on the Mall in Washington. It is the headquarters of the Smithsonian Institution. There are also many other buildings. They are filled with more than 65 million unusual and exciting objects that tell of our nation's history. It would take years to see them all.

In 1980, the name of the National Museum of History and Technology was changed to the National Museum of American History. It has one of the noisiest exhibits in Washington. It is caused by a recording of the sounds made by a locomotive.

You can see the real Star-Spangled Banner Flag in Flag Hall. Francis Scott Key wrote our national anthem because of this flag.

Some things to see in the National Museum of American History: a 1913 Model T Ford (above left), the original Star-Spangled Banner (above), and the Foucault Pendulum (left).

The first thing you see when you walk in is the 71½-foot Foucault Pendulum (FOE • callt PEN • joo • lum). The pendulum never stops; it is always moving. This is proof that the earth is rotating.

This huge museum shows the growth of America over the last 200 years.

Uncle Beasley, a life-size model of a dinosaur (Triceratops), greets visitors who enter the National Museum of Natural History. It is a friendly dinosaur made of fiberglass. It may be a relative of the dinosaurs who used to live in Washington.

Murals, exhibits, and displays tell the story of our planet over billions of years since it was formed.

The National Air and Space Museum is filled with exciting exhibits. They show the progress made in man's adventures with flying.

Kitty Hawk, the plane that made the first successful flight, is the first thing you see when you walk in. The Spirit of St. Louis is there, too. It's the plane Charles Lindbergh used to fly across the Atlantic Ocean alone. It was the first time anyone had ever done that.

The spacecraft that took the astronauts to the moon in the Apollo Program is also on display.

The National Air and Space Museum's Milestones of Flight
Hall. Above are the X-15 jet, the Wright Brothers' Kitty
Hawk plane, and Charles Lindbergh's Spirit of St. Louis;
below is the Apollo II spacecraft that went to the moon.

The National Zoo welcomes millions of visitors every year. The zoo has 165 acres in the heart of Rock Creek Park. Over 2500 animals live there. Here is the home of Smokey the Bear. Smokey is an American Black bear who looks brown. Smokey was saved from a forest fire by rangers in New Mexico.

You can visit Ling-Ling and Hsing-Hsing, the giant Panda bears who live in a special house. They were a gift to the children of America from the People's Republic of China. Two other famous residents of the zoo are Priya and Bharat, two female white tigers. They are the granddaughters of Mohine, the famous white tiger obtained by the zoo from the Maharajah of Rewa.

Ham, the Space Chimp, once lived at the zoo. He made a space flight about a month before Alan Shepard. He followed the same flight plan. Ham had to respond to signals and check out the controls. He had a perfect flight. Good work, Ham. Ham now lives at the North Carolina Zoo.

The National Zoo is home to white tigers (above), Smokey the Bear (above right), and giant pandas (below left). Ham, the Space Chimp, (below right) once lived there, too.

On the Virginia side of the Potomac River is Arlington
National Cemetery. The Tomb of The Unknown Soldier
is here.

Some Washington sights across the Potomac River:
the Tomb of the Unknown Soldier (above),
President John F. Kennedy's grave (above right),
and the Custis-Lee mansion (below right)
at Arlington National Cemetery, and
Mount Vernon (below).

This grave honors every man who died unknown in every war that the United States fought in. On the tomb is written "Here Rests In Honored Glory An American Soldier Known But To God." One armed service man paces out a guard of honor in front of the Tomb. Every hour on the hour the guard is changed. Try to visit at the right time to see the "Changing of the Guard."

Arlington House, called the "Custis-Lee Mansion," is in the middle of the cemetery. On the hillside below is the grave of President John Fitzgerald Kennedy. An Eternal Flame burns on his grave. The grave of the president's brother, Senator Robert F. Kennedy, is nearby. Both brothers were killed by assassins.

Washington's home, Mount Vernon, is in Virginia. You will enjoy visiting his home and the beautiful grounds.

Washington, D.C., is full of many things to see and do. Museums and government buildings are only part of Washington's treasures. There are many more.

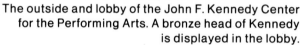
The outside and lobby of the John F. Kennedy Center for the Performing Arts. A bronze head of Kennedy is displayed in the lobby.

At the John F. Kennedy Center for the Performing Arts, the Young People's Concerts of the National Symphony Orchestra are given. The Kennedy Center is a living memorial to our late president.

In the United States Botanic Garden you can be in a tropical jungle one minute seeing tall palm trees and plants, and be in a hot desert the next minute.

At Explorer's Hall on the first floor of the National Geographic Society the world, past and present, can be explored. Here you can see a great model of the solar system.

Embassy Row is on Massachusetts Avenue. More than a hundred foreign nations have embassies here. The flags of their countries are flying in front of their buildings. It is a beautiful sight!

Washington is so filled with history, past and present, that you can feel it in the air.

What happens here affects every citizen, and, often the whole world.

As history comes to life before your eyes it makes you proud and happy to be part of it all—proud to be an American! Proud of your capital city, Washington, D.C.!

Aerial view of "The Hill"

Facts About the DISTRICT OF COLUMBIA

Area—68 square miles
Highest Point—88 feet
Lowest Point—Sea Level
Temperature Records—high: 106°; low: minus 15°
Population—637,651 (1980 census)
Population Density—10,127 persons per square mile
Principal Cities—Boundary of the city of Washington is
   the same as that of the District of Columbia
Motto—*Justitia Omnibus* (Justice for All)
Flower—American Beauty Rose
Tree—Scarlet Oak
Bird—Wood Thrush

District of Columbia History

1608—Captain John Smith visits District of Columbia area.
1622—Captain Henry Fleete first European to live in what is now District of
   Columbia.
1789—Georgetown University founded.
1790—Congress passes act establishing permanent U.S. capital city.
1791—President George Washington chooses location of District of
   Columbia; capital city named after him.
1792—Pierre L'Enfant designs plans for capital city; construction begins on
   President's House.
1793—George Washington lays Capitol cornerstone.
1800—Congress meets in new Capitol for first time; John Adams first
   President to reside in President's House; Library of Congress
   established. First newspapers begin publication.
1801—Thomas Jefferson first President inaugurated in District of Columbia.

1802—City of Washington chartered.
1807—First black school opened. It was taught by a white man.
1814—During War of 1812 British burn Capitol and President's House; latter
   painted white to hide scars of fire, becomes known as the White House.
1821—Columbia College (later to become George Washington University)
   opens.
1827—Capitol completed thirty-four years after cornerstone laid.
1828—Construction begun on Chesapeake and Ohio Canal.
1844—Samuel F.B. Morse sends first telegraph message from Capitol
   basement.

1846—Smithsonian Institution established by Congress.

1864—Arlington National Cemetery established in Virginia across Potomac River from Washington.

1865—Abraham Lincoln assassinated in Ford's Theatre

1867—Howard University founded for Negro education.

1868—Andrew Johnson first President to be impeached by House of Representatives; conviction vote fails in Senate.

1887—L'Enfant's plans for city rediscovered and extended.

1888—555-feet-high Washington Monument opened to public four years after completion and forty years after construction began.

1895—Georgetown becomes part of Washington.

1901—Plans for The Mall developed.

1912—Japanese cherry trees planted along Tidal Basin.

1921—Tomb of Unknown Soldier dedicated in Arlington National Cemetery.

1922—Lincoln Memorial dedicated.

1926—National Capital Park and Planning Commission created.

1927—National Arboretum established on Anacostia River. First Cherry Blossom Festival held.

1932—World War I veterans camp out in Washington demanding bonuses for wartime service; riot erupts when Army removes them.

1935—U.S. Supreme Court building completed.

1941—National Gallery of Art opens.

1943—Jefferson Memorial dedicated; Pentagon construction completed.

1951—Gutting and reconstruction of interior of White House completed.

1960—Front of Capitol extended.

1961—Twenty-third amendment to Constitution gives D.C. residents right to vote in Presidential elections.

1963—More than 200,000 persons gather in Washington for civil rights demonstration.

1964—Blair House opened as President's guest house.

1967—First black mayor of Washington, Walter E. Washington, appointed.

1968—Fires and looting sweep Washington (and other U.S. cities) after assassination of civil rights leader Dr. Martin Luther King, Jr.

1969—Quarter of a million persons march on Washington protesting Vietnam War.

1970—District of Columbia given one non-voting delegate to House of Representatives.

1971—Terrorist bomb explodes inside Capitol; Kennedy Center for the Performing Arts opens.

1974—Mormon Temple opens; Richard Nixon first president to resign office.

1976—Capital city is center of nationwide Bicentennial celebration.

1978—East building of National Gallery of Art opens.

1979—Project restoring historic Georgetown underway.

1980—Vietnam Veterans National Memorial is dedicated

INDEX

About the Author:

Mrs. Lumley is a nationally known reading specialist and author of numerous books and articles on reading and its teaching. experience includes teaching at all levels from elementary through university classes, and director of the Reading Center for the W ington, D.C. Public Schools. Mrs. Lumley is a member of the board of directors of Reading is Fundamental (RIF). She is also a Tru of the Williamsport (Pa.) Area Community College and is an active participant in leading professional associations.

About the Artists:

Len Meents studied painting and drawing at Southern Illinois University and after graduation in 1969 he moved to Chicago. Meents works full time as a painter and illustrator. He and his wife and child currently make their home in LaGrange, Illinois.

Richard Wahl, graduate of the Art Center College of Design in Los Angeles has illustrated a number of magazine articles and be lets. He is a skilled artist and photographer who advocates realistic interpretations of his subjects. He lives with his wife and two sor Libertyville, Illinois.